HOT TOPICS

WITHDRAWN

DESIGNER BABIES

McHenry Public Library District
809 N. Front Street
McHenry, IL 60050

John Bliss

Chicago, Illinois

www.heinemannraintree.com
Visit our website to find out
more information about
Heinemann-Raintree books.

To order:
☎ Phone 888-454-2279
🖨 Visit www.heinemannraintree.com
to browse our catalog and order online.

© 2012 Heinemann Library
an imprint of Capstone Global Library, LLC
Chicago, Illinois

Visit our website at
www.heinemannraintree.com

Edited by Adam Miller, Andrew Farrow, and
Jennifer Locke
Designed by Clare Webber and Steven Mead
Original illustrations © Capstone Global Library
Ltd.
Illustrated by KJA-Artists.com and Art
Construction
Picture research by Ruth Blair
Production by Eirian Griffiths
Originated by Capstone Global Library Ltd.
Printed and bound in China by Leo Paper Group
Ltd.

16 15 14 13 12
10 9 8 7 6 5 4 3 2 1

**Library of Congress Cataloging-in-Publication
Data**
Bliss, John.
  Designer babies / John Bliss.
      p. cm.—(Hot topics)
  Includes bibliographical references
and index.
  ISBN 978-1-4329-4870-2 (hc)
1. Human reproductive technology.
2. Preimplantation genetic diagnosis.
3. Genetic screening. I. Title.
  RG133.5.B65 2012
  616.6'920642—dc22
                2010044360

Acknowledgments
The author and publishers are grateful to the
following for permission to reproduce copyright
material: Alamy pp. **4** (© AF archive), **6**
(© Trinity Mirror/Mirrorpix), **9** (© Pictorial Press,
Ltd.), **26** (© UpperCut Images), **31** (© Urban
Zone), **33** (© Penny Tweedie), **35** (© Ingram
Publishing), **39** (© ARISTIDIS VAFEIADAKIS), **40**
(© ITAR-TASS Photo Agency), **42** (© Pictorial
Press, Ltd.); Corbis pp. **11** (© Bettmann), **16**
(© Owen Franken), **19** (© Tomas Rodriguez), **28**
(© Ed Kashi), **41** (© Charles W. Luzier/Reuters);
Getty Images pp. **15** (Jason Mitchell/BuzzFoto/
FilmMagic), **21** (AFP), **23** (Robyn Beck/AFP),
25 (Robyn Beck/AFP); PA Photos pp. **13** (Chris
Radburn/PA Archive), **37** John Giles/PA Archive);
Shutterstock pp. **27** (© DD Coral), **43**
(© FLariviere), **44** (© Denise Campione);
The Kobal Collection p. **7** (GAUMONT); p. **17**
Wellcome Library (Rama Knight).

Cover photograph of toy babies reproduced
with the permission of Science Photo Library
(Lawrence Lawry).

We would like to thank Kristen Kowalkowski for
her invaluable help in the preparation of this
book.

Disclaimer
All the Internet addresses (URLs) given in this
book were valid at the time of going to press.
However, due to the dynamic nature of the
Internet, some addresses may have changed,
or sites may have changed or ceased to exist
since publication. While the author and publisher
regret any inconvenience this may cause readers,
no responsibility for any such changes can be
accepted by either the author or the publisher.

CONTENTS

Some words are printed in bold, **like this**. You can find out what they mean by looking in the glossary.

WHAT ARE DESIGNER BABIES?

■ Boris Karloff, who played Dr. Frankenstein's monster in the 1931 film, set the standard for all later interpretations.

"It's alive! Alive!"

These are the words of Dr. Frankenstein as the creature he has built starts to twitch on the operating table. Frankenstein has pieced together his creation from corpses dug up in the dead of night. He has placed a new brain into the giant skull. And now, as a storm rages overhead, he uses electricity to animate the body. Finally, it begins to move. Frankenstein has created a new human being.

From *Frankenstein* to *Young Frankenstein*, hundreds of science-fiction stories and movies have dealt with the mad scientist creating life in the laboratory. The stories are no longer science fiction, and the scientist is no longer mad. "Designer babies" are right around the corner.

Designing children

For most of human history, having children has been a matter of chance. Men and women reproduce, and the results are left to nature. People may choose who they marry with an eye to what their children will look like, but the actual results are out of their hands.

With so little control over the situation, most expectant parents say they don't care what their baby looks like, "as long as it's healthy." But secretly, they often have a dream baby in mind. They fantasize about playing catch or kicking around a football with their son. Or they dream about going shopping or having tea parties with their daughter. They may hope their child has his mother's eyes or his father's chin. Perhaps they want her to have her father's hair or her mother's personality.

These dreams of creating the "perfect" child may not be far off. Even today, advances in **genetic** science are giving parents more control over the **traits**, or physical characteristics, their children inherit. **Embryos** can be screened for diseases carried in the **genes**, such as **hemophilia**, a blood disorder. Some fertility clinics even give parents the choice of whether they want a boy or a girl.

Journalists use the term *designer baby* to refer to children whose genetic traits are chosen by parents or doctors. This developing technology offers great benefits but also a range of ethical considerations. Right now, parents can't choose physical traits, such as hair or eye color. But those possibilities are not far off. Eventually, we will have the ability to create new and improved genes. As the technology develops, the question will change from "What can be done?" to "What should be done?"

Modern birth science

As recently as 50 years ago, the idea of scientists designing human beings was the material of fantasy. In his 1932 novel *Brave New World*, author Aldous Huxley imagined a world in which all children are created in a factory. Though we are far from that future, recent advances in birth science would have seemed like fantasy to Huxley's readers.

The road to designer babies begins with the birth of Louise Brown in the United Kingdom in 1978. Though Louise appeared to be a normal infant, her life began in a new way. She was the first embryo successfully conceived outside of the womb. The press trumpeted Louise as the first "test tube baby." In reality, after her embryo was created, Louise grew inside her mother's womb, just like any other baby.

Louise Brown was conceived through a process called **in vitro fertilization** (IVF). In the 30 years since her birth, science has made huge strides. Now fertility clinics around the world help parents conceive through IVF. Some clinics even let parents choose the gender of their child.

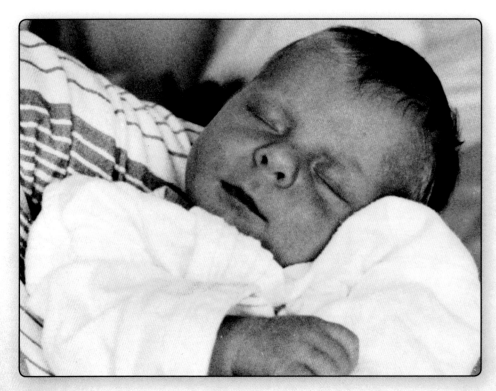

■ When Louise Brown was born in 1978, she made headlines around the world as the first "test tube baby."

We have continued to learn about genes and **chromosomes**, the building blocks of all life. Genes and chromosomes are described more in the next chapter. We now have a much deeper understanding of how genes work and interact with each other. In 2003 an international team of scientists completed mapping the human **genome**. This is the series of all the genes in the human body. This has led to advances in gene therapy, a way of altering genes to combat genetic diseases. This gene "map" also gives scientists the information they need to select specific physical traits for these new designer babies.

The study of how physical characteristics are passed from one generation to another is called genetics. This science has gone beyond merely identifying genes. Today genetic **engineers** are actually replacing genes in plants and animals to give them specially designed characteristics. Genetically modified plants and animals are already a part of many farms. People wonder if genetically modified humans will be next.

Science fiction often paints horrifying visions of the future of genetic science. Some critics of this research have similar concerns. But for a growing number of doctors, researchers, and ordinary parents, birth science is something they experience every day. In considering the ethics of human genetics, we need to look at the issues both rationally and emotionally. What we think and feel about these new developments are both important.

■ The 2010 thriller *Splice* tells the story of two genetic engineers who create a new life form by blending human and animal DNA. In the movie, the experiment has deadly repercussions.

HOW DOES IT WORK?

While the actual process of creating a designer baby is complex, the science behind it is fairly straightforward. All of our physical characteristics—and perhaps some mental and emotional ones as well—are carried on structures called chromosomes within our cells. Each chromosome contains a series of genes that determine individual characteristics, such as height or hair color. During reproduction, a set of chromosomes from each parent is combined in the fertilized egg. The goal of the genetic scientist is to combine the genes that carry selected traits.

CONTROVERSIAL TERMINOLOGY

Although we use the term "designer babies" throughout this book, many professionals in the field find the term offensive. They point out that no matter how a child comes into existence, its parents will love it no less than had it been **conceived** completely naturally. They accuse journalists of using scare tactics, such as sensational headlines or biased sources, to sell their stories. Journalists defend the term as a simple way of describing the issue. In any case, the term is in wide use.

Choosing traits

Selecting for best traits is nothing new. Farmers have been breeding crops and animals for their physical characteristics for thousands of years. Even before people understood how genes worked, they were breeding plants and animals that were stronger, healthier, or produced more food. Sometimes, scientists breed together two different kinds of plants or animals to make a new creature. A mule is the offspring of a horse and a donkey. Farmers often cross-pollinate plants to combine their best qualities.

CASE STUDY

Gregor Mendel

The science of genetics begins with an Austrian monk named Gregor Mendel. During the 1850s, Mendel studied pea plants to learn how they passed on their physical traits, such as height and seed color. When he bred a tall plant with a short plant, he got all tall plants. But when he bred those new tall plants together, he got some tall plants and some short plants. As he continued to breed plants, he saw that he grew three tall plants for every one short plant. Mendel realized that something in the plant—later called a gene—was passing on these traits.

■ Gregor Mendel is called the Father of Genetics.

■ This chart shows how genes combine to produce different traits. Pea plants can be either tall or short. One tall (T) and one short (t) gene results in tall plants. Only when two genes for short plants (tt) are present will the plant be short.

	T	t
T	TT	Tt
t	Tt	tt

CASE STUDY

Buck v. Bell

For some critics, the idea of genetic selection raises the specter of **eugenics**. This movement, which arose in the late nineteenth century, supported improving the human race through selective breeding. The concept of eugenics grew out of the ideas of **natural selection** put forth by Charles Darwin. In fact, Francis Galton, the British scientist who developed and named the concept, was Darwin's cousin.

By the early twentieth century, interest in eugenics had spread throughout the world. "Positive eugenics" focused on supporting people who were perceived as "good stock." "Fitter Family" and "Better Baby" contests awarded prizes to families judged to be good examples of health and hygiene. There was a dark side, though. The practice of "negative eugenics" sought to **sterilize** those seen as "bad stock," to keep them from reproducing. This dark side reached its peak with the practices of Nazi Germany, in which millions of people who were judged "unfit," because of their race or sexuality, were put to death.

In the United States, the conflict over eugenics came to a head with the case of Buck v. Bell. Carrie Buck was a patient at a mental institution in Virginia. Buck's doctor claimed that Buck had a mental age of nine. Buck's mother was also mentally challenged. Buck's doctor sought to have her sterilized, saying that she represented a "genetic threat" to society. Buck's legal guardian appealed the case, and in May 1927 it was argued before the Supreme Court.

In an 8–1 ruling, the Court agreed that Carrie Buck should be sterilized. Justice Oliver Wendell Holmes, Jr. wrote the decision. Holmes was one of the most respected justices to ever serve on the Court, but many people disagreed with him in this case.

■ Oliver Wendell Holmes around the time of Buck v. Bell. His ruling shows that he lacked a true understanding of genetic science.

In letting the law stand, he wrote, "It is better for all the world, if instead of waiting to execute degenerate offspring for crime, or to let them starve for their imbecility, society can prevent those who are manifestly unfit from continuing their kind." In other words, Holmes thought it was better to sterilize people who had what he considered "bad" genes rather than let them have children who might be unable to take care of themselves.

By the end of World War II, eugenics had fallen out of favor in most countries. In 1942, the U.S. Supreme Court struck down a law that allowed the sterilization of criminals. Though this put an end to most eugenics practices, Virginia's law remained on the books until 1974, when it was finally repealed.

In vitro fertilization

At present, the only way to select specific genetic traits in humans is by using embryos that have been created through in vitro fertilization (IVF). Genes are not manipulated directly. Instead, a number of eggs are fertilized, and the resulting embryos are then scanned for the appropriate traits. This process, called **pre-implantation genetic diagnosis**, is discussed in the next section.

In IVF, human egg cells are fertilized outside the **womb**. The term *in vitro* is Latin for "within the glass." Despite the use of the phrase *test tube babies* for children conceived through IVF, the embryos are neither conceived nor developed in test tubes. Instead, fertilization usually occurs in a petri dish or other laboratory instrument containing a substance, called a **culture** that promotes growth. Once several embryos have been created, one or more are implanted into the mother's womb, where they develop until they are born.

In vitro fertilization is not a perfect science. Less than half of embryos that are implanted result in live births. On the other hand, many women impregnated through IVF have multiple births. There are several reasons for this. During natural conception, usually only one fertilized egg grows in the womb. Because of the low success rate in IVF, multiple embryos are usually implanted. In addition, women undergoing IVF often take fertility drugs to assist the process.

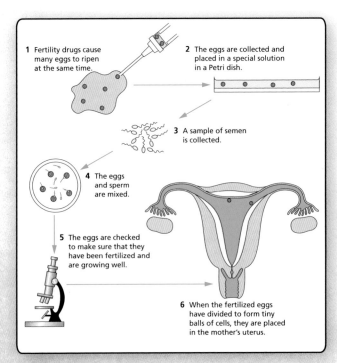

1 Fertility drugs cause many eggs to ripen at the same time.

2 The eggs are collected and placed in a special solution in a Petri dish.

3 A sample of semen is collected.

4 The eggs and sperm are mixed.

5 The eggs are checked to make sure that they have been fertilized and are growing well.

6 When the fertilized eggs have divided to form tiny balls of cells, they are placed in the mother's uterus.

■ During in vitro fertilization, an egg from the mother is fertilized in the lab and then placed into the mother's womb.

CASE STUDY

Louise Brown

Louise Brown was literally born famous. That's because she was the first baby to be conceived using in vitro fertilization.

Louise was born on July 25, 1978. Her parents, Lesley and John Brown, had been trying to have a baby for nine years. But Lesley had blocked **Fallopian tubes**, which kept her eggs from descending properly. In 1976 she was referred to Dr. Patrick Steptoe. Steptoe and his partner, Dr. Robert Edwards, performed the still experimental procedure.

Minutes after Louise was born, she was in front of television cameras. Everyone wanted to see this new miracle of modern science. Since then, the media has regularly intruded into her life.

But Louise has grown up surprisingly well adjusted. Her parents worked to give her a normal life. Eventually, she got married and had a child of her own.

■ Louise Brown was the first child born through in vitro fertilization. In 2006 she gave birth to a boy after a natural conception.

CASE STUDY

Nadya Suleman

Nadya Suleman came to the attention of the media when she gave birth to **octuplets**, or eight babies, in January 2009. Suleman was quickly dubbed "octomom" by the press.

The Suleman octuplets are a result of the multiple embryos that were implanted during her IVF procedure. Because not all embryos develop into viable fetuses, it is not unusual for doctors to implant more than one. As the public later discovered, though, Suleman had six other children, who were also conceived through IVF. In addition, she was 33 when she underwent IVF treatment. In general, women of her age should not receive more than three implants. Suleman's doctor came under criticism for implanting as many embryos as he did. The following October, he was expelled from the American Society for Reproductive Medicine.

In her defense, Suleman claimed that the embryos she had implanted were a result of her previous IVF sessions. She claimed she had the remaining embryos implanted to save them from being destroyed. She also claimed that she had six embryos implanted, but that two of the embryos later split, producing two sets of twins. Later, both of these claims turned out to be false.

Many people felt Suleman should never have been allowed to have the procedure, since she already had so many children at home. When it turned out that she was unemployed, divorced, and living with her parents, the public was outraged. They felt both Suleman and her doctor acted irresponsibly.

WHAT DO YOU THINK?

How would you feel if you learned you were conceived through IVF? Would it change how you thought about yourself? Why?

Ethical problems of IVF

Suleman's case points out some of the ethical concerns surrounding IVF. Multiple implants often result in multiple births, causing both a financial and health strain on the mother and her family.

Multiple eggs are fertilized during the process, in order to create more than one viable embryo. Extra embryos may be destroyed. This creates a moral problem for those who believe that life begins at conception. In their eyes, these "extra" embryos are human lives. Often the extra embryos are frozen, to be used in later procedures, if necessary. Critics of IVF don't see this as much better than destroying the embryos. Freezing can also cause disputes over who "owns" these embryos.

■ Nadya Suleman's multiple births thrust the ethical issues of IVF into public scrutiny.

In cases of multiple pregnancies, one or more of the extra fetuses are often removed, in a process called selective reduction. Critics charge that this is nothing less than abortion and equate it to murder.

PGD

Pre-implantation genetic diagnosis (PGD) is at the heart of the designer baby process. This method is used to screen the genetic makeup of embryos created during in vitro fertilization. It is often used by couples whose children might be at risk for disorders that are carried in the genes, such as Down syndrome or **hemophilia**.

Embryos screened through PGD are fertilized as usual through the IVF process. Once the embryo has grown to the eight-cell stage, a doctor removes one or two cells and examines the **DNA**, or genetic information, of these cells under a microscope. The doctor is looking for markers for specific genetic disorders, especially ones that run in the families of the parents. Embryos carrying the markers for disease are discarded. Only normal embryos are then implanted in the womb.

Some genetic disorders are specific to one gender or another. Hemophilia, for example, affects boys more than girls. If a family has a history of hemophilia, the couple may choose to select only female embryos.

At present, PGD is only used to screen embryos for disease. In the near future, though, it may be possible to screen for other traits, such as height or intelligence. Many people worry about the implications of screening for physical or personality traits. These ethical questions are discussed more fully in the next chapter.

■ Specialized equipment is used to scan embryos during PGD.

CASE STUDY

The Human Genome Project

In order to screen for genetic traits, you need to know where to find them. Our genetic makeup, or genome, is stored on 46 chromosomes located in the nucleus of every cell. During reproduction, the fertilized egg receives 23 chromosomes from each parent. Scientists have understood this for years. But until recently, the location of specific genes on particular chromosomes was unknown.

In 1990 scientists set about mapping this genetic information. The project was initially headed up by James Watson, who had worked on exploring the structure of DNA in the 1950s. Eventually, though, this became an international study, made up of scientists from the United States, Great Britain, Japan, and other nations.

In April 2003 the work of mapping the genome was completed. The information discovered through the Human Genome Project makes designer babies possible. Gene sequencing revealed which chromosomes contained genes for which traits. While initial results of the study were published in 2006, scientists continue to study the data. They learn more about how genes work and how to use this information to fight disease.

■ The human genome is so long that the printed information covers more than a hundred volumes.

Gender selection

Some clinics go beyond screening for genetic disorders. They offer parents the opportunity to choose the sex of their unborn child. This is relatively easy to do. In human beings, gender is determined by a combination of X and Y chromosomes. Females have two X chromosomes, while males have one X and one Y. Laboratory technicians use equipment to separate embryos into XX and XY. Only embryos of the desired gender are implanted into the mother.

Scientists began studying gender selection in the 1980s. Originally, it was used as a way to screen for genetic disorders. Today, though, some couples are offered this service as a method of "family balancing." A family with one or more boys, for example, may choose to only select girl embryos.

Gender selection raises ethical questions. In some cultures, such as those of China and India, boys are valued more than girls. Boys carry on the family name and are seen as more likely to have the income to support their parents. Some fear that gender selection will throw those societies even more out of balance.

Even in Western countries, though, many women face gender bias. People who oppose gender selection fear that allowing people to choose the sex of their baby will increase this bias. People in favor of sex selection for family balancing say it will only be used by parents who already have one or more child of one gender.

In the United Kingdom and other European countries, sex selection for any purpose other than gender-related illness is against the law. This hasn't stopped families who want to use sex selection for family balancing. They simply travel to the United States for the procedure, where it is not regulated.

"Sex selection is sex discrimination, and I don't think that is ethical. It's not ethical to take someone off the street and help them have a boy or a girl."

Dr. James Grifo, the Society for Assisted Reproductive Technology

MICROSORT

The Genetics & IVF Institute in Fairfax, Virginia, offers family balancing through sorting sperm rather than selecting from fertilized eggs. X chromosomes carry slightly more genetic material than Y chromosomes. Because of this, it is possible to separate X and Y sperm using specialized equipment. The process, called MicroSort, has a high rate of success in determining gender. MicroSort avoids some of the ethical problems people have with destroying embryos created for IVF. Since only embryos of the proper gender are created in the first place, fewer embryos are destroyed overall.

■ Some parents use gender selection as a way of balancing the number of boys and girls in their family.

CASE STUDY

Fertility Institutes

In February 2009 the Fertility Institutes, a fertility clinic with locations in the United States and Mexico, found itself in the middle of an international controversy. The Institutes announced that it planned to offer services that would allow parents to choose their baby's hair, eye, and skin colors. The announcement set off a flurry of news stories and blog posts on both sides of the Atlantic, many of which condemned the Institutes. Mark Hughes, a doctor who uses the PGD process himself, said that "no legitimate lab would get into it [trait selection] and, if they did, they'd be **ostracized**." Within a month, the Institutes announced that it had reconsidered and would not offer the service after all.

Prior to the announcement, the Fertility Institutes was just one of many fertility clinics in operation around the world. Such clinics work with couples who have been unsuccessful at having children on their own. The Institutes offers a variety of services, including fertility testing for both women and men and assisted reproductive treatments. Assisted reproduction simply means techniques used to help a woman become pregnant. The Institutes offer in vitro fertilization and several related services as well. The company's motto is "Helping Couples Become Families."

No stranger to controversy

Even before it announced plans to let parents select traits such as hair and eye color, the Fertility Institutes offered some controversial services. For example, the clinic is a leading provider in **surrogacy** services. A surrogate is a woman who carries a fetus for couples who cannot reproduce on their own. The Institutes recruits women who are willing to become surrogates and even offers surrogacy to gay couples who wish to have children.

Like many clinics, the Institutes offers embryo screening through PGD to nearly all of its patients. Even couples with a history of genetic disorders are offered those services. Most of its PGD work involves screening for gender, and the company advertises that it is the worldwide leader in gender selection.

WHAT DO YOU THINK?

Surrogacy involves hiring a woman to carry a child who at birth is given to the sponsoring couple. Do you agree with such an arrangement? Does it make a difference if the couple hiring the surrogate are heterosexuals or homosexuals?

Indeed, the Institutes draws its clientele from around the world. Information on its website regarding sex selection and family balancing is available in English, Chinese, French, and German. The company partners with a travel agency, World O'Travel, to offer travel arrangements for its international customers. Even before the latest controversy, the Fertility Institutes was in the news as a destination for couples from around the world who came to the clinic for its gender selection services. In one week, the clinic consulted with patients from China, Germany, Canada, the Czech Republic, Guam, Mexico, and New Zealand.

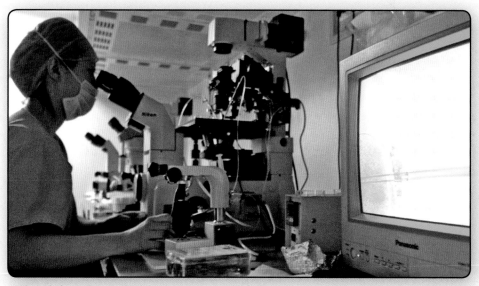

■ Founded in 1986, the Fertility Institutes now has facilities in New York, Los Angeles, and Guadalajara, Mexico.

Trait selection

Any previous controversy the Fertility Institutes had been involved in was calm compared to what happened in early February 2009. That's when the company announced it was expanding its PGD services. Along with gender selection, it would start offering parents the opportunity to choose some physical traits, such as eye and hair color. For many geneticists, this was not a surprise. The science of trait selection had been growing, and the ability to screen for more than genetic disorders was on the horizon. Dr. Jeffrey Steinberg, head of the Fertility Institutes, told the BBC, "I would not say this is a dangerous road. It's an uncharted road." And the Institutes was prepared to be the first clinic to go down that road.

Not everyone believed that the Fertility Institutes had the technology to offer traits selection. Dr. Arthur Caplan, director of the Center for **Bioethics** at the University of Pennsylvania, told CBS news, "I think he's wrong. I don't think we're going to get to eye color and hair color and freckles for a couple more years." But even Caplan admitted that trait selection was coming. He continued, "We're headed that way. It is going to be possible to pick traits, not because of diseases or avoiding dysfunction, but because somebody has a taste for a particular child or a preference for a particular child."

Though some people were happy with the Institutes' announcement, most were not. The magazine *Scientific American* called for more regulation over reproductive technologies and said that trait selections would lead to "Build-A-Bear" babies. Critic Wesley J. Smith, who often examines ethical issues, wrote, "No 'right' is absolute. The time has long since passed to put some regulatory controls over the wild, wild west of IVF." Even the pope weighed in. On February 21, 2009, he condemned the "obsessive search for the perfect child." He continued, "A new mentality is creeping in that tends to justify a different consideration of life and personal dignity."

On February 28, Steinberg continued to defend his position. He told London's *Sunday Telegraph*, "I understand the … concerns, but we cannot escape the fact that science is moving forward. If I have to get smacked around by people who think it is inappropriate, then I'm willing to live with that."

Two days later, though, Steinberg changed his position. The Fertility Institutes posted a press release on its website that said, "In response to feedback received related to our plans to introduce preimplantation genetic prediction of eye pigmentation, an internal, self regulatory decision has been made to proceed no further with this project." It went on to say that the decision was due to "public perception" and the "apparent negative societal impacts involved."

Still, the services offered by the Institutes are obviously right around the corner. The technology to select physical traits is available, and Steinberg believes "it's time for everyone to pull their heads out of the sand." Sooner or later, the Fertility Institutes or another clinic will offer trait selection.

■ Dr. Jeffrey Steinberg, the director of the Fertility Institutes, has been active in the field of IVF for more than 30 years.

THE GROWING CONTROVERSY

As the case of the Fertility Institutes makes clear, the possibility of parents choosing the genetic makeup of their child is no longer something out of science fiction. It is something that will be happening in just a few short years. As this possibility looms, arguments for and against the practice have heated up. Dozens of articles, editorials, and even books have appeared on the subject. Thoughtful points are made on both sides of the debate. The only thing people can agree on is that the issue cannot be ignored.

A private matter

Many people think that any decision about genetic selection is private and should remain between the parents and their doctor. When in vitro fertilization was first introduced, many people rejected it as unnatural. Today it is accepted. Most people consider IVF a private matter.

This is the attitude that Dr. Jeffrey Steinberg of the Fertility Institutes takes. He sees genetic selection as a matter of science and service. As a doctor, he says he wants to provide all of the benefits of science to his patients. He sees no difference between screening embryos for genetic disorders and screening them for physical traits, such as height or hair color. Others see a danger in considering some genetic traits as "better" than others. They worry about a culture in which some traits are prized more than others.

Even if genetic selection is a private choice, the decision raises some of the same concerns presented by IVF. At present, the only way to select for a specific combination of traits—such as hair color, eye color, and height—would be to create hundreds of embryos and screen them all for the right combination. The more specific you are about the traits you want, the fewer embryos are likely to qualify. This would result in a huge number of embryos being destroyed.

Many people who believe the ultimate decision rests with the parents still recognize the number of issues involved. They say that few parents have the knowledge to make such a choice, so they recommend that parents go through counseling before making any decisions.

THE ROLE OF GOVERNMENT

Since 1991 genetic medicine in the United Kingdom has been overseen by the Human Fertilisation and Embryology Authority (HFEA). The HFEA licenses and regulates fertility clinics and hospitals that offer in vitro fertilization and other methods of assisting parents with conceiving a child. It also has control over human embryo research. The HFEA has strict guidelines about which procedures patients can receive. For example, parents in the United Kingdom are generally not offered sex selection.

In 2010 the British government announced plans to dissolve the HFEA and fold its functions into other government organizations. Some doubt the reorganization will ever occur. Even if it does, the government is likely to retain some control over regulating clinics and procedures. The role that government should play in making reproductive choices continues to be debated in many nations.

■ Vials holding eggs belonging to hundreds of clients from around the world are housed in a room at the offices of The Fertility Institute in Encino, California. Besides couples from the U.S., people from China, Hong Kong, Singapore, Thailand, Japan, Germany, Britain, and Canada come to Steinberg's clinics.

Medicine or marketing?

Supporters of genetic selection compare it to plastic surgery. Just as patients can choose to have surgery to give them the appearance they want, they say parents should have the right to choose the genetic makeup of their child. But where do you draw the line between medicine and business? Doctors like Steinberg want to provide the best possible service for their patients. At what point do patients become customers? Is everything and anything for sale at the fertility clinic?

One obvious difference between plastic surgery and genetic selection is choice. The patient who undergoes plastic surgery chooses to have his or her looks altered. The child whose genes are selected by the parents has no choice in the matter. The rights of unborn children are hotly debated and will come up again in this discussion. In this case, much of the child's future has been decided while he or she is still an embryo.

At the same time, buying and selling genetic material is nothing new. Since IVF was introduced in the late 1970s, a booming market for healthy egg and sperm cells has developed. Over the past 30 years, the growth of **artificial insemination** has turned prospective parents into consumers. People are willing to pay top dollar for reproductive cells from suitable sources.

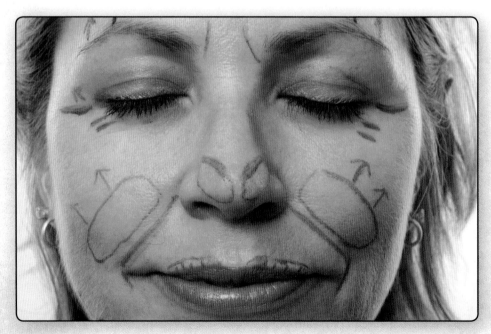

■ Supporters say choosing a child's traits is no different than using plastic surgery to change your own appearance.

Some customers are quite up front with their demands. Not long ago, one such customer ran ads in the school newspapers of top universities. The advertiser was looking for an egg from a woman who was at least five feet ten inches tall and athletic, who had no major family medical problems, and who scored well on her college entrance exams. The ad offered $50,000 to the proper donor.

In 1999 a fashion photographer launched a website on which he offered eggs from models featured on the site. The eggs were available for auction, with starting bids of $15,000 to $150,000. On the site, the photographer wrote, "'If you could increase the chance of reproducing beautiful children, and thus giving them an advantage in society, would you?" This is the question faced by **consumers** of genetic material.

Some people have no problem with selling eggs and sperm cells in this way. They say that if there is a market for it, sales should continue. Others find the idea distasteful. For them, selling genetic material is little better than selling human beings. They believe some things should be off-limit.

WHAT DO YOU THINK?

Are you against buying or selling reproductive cells? How would you feel if you learned that you were born as a result of a purchased egg or sperm cell?

■ Those who oppose genetic marketing say you shouldn't choose a child as you would a new car.

CASE STUDY

Genetic banking

A **cryobank**, also called a sperm bank, is a facility that collects and stores human sperm to be used in artificial insemination. In most cases, the sperm are used by a woman who is not the donor's spouse. It may be used by a single woman or by married couples in which the male is **infertile**. Note that while men who contribute their sperm are called donors, they are generally paid. *Cryo* refers to freezing, and the sperm at these facilities are frozen to preserve them.

California Cryobank is one of the world's leading sperm banks. The facility's main location is in Palo Alto, California, which is near Stanford University. Another office is located in Cambridge, Massachusetts, near the well-known universities Harvard and Massachusetts Institute of Technology (MIT). The company has chosen these locations because it recruits its donors from college campuses. It runs ads in campus newspapers and offers up to $900 a month in compensation.

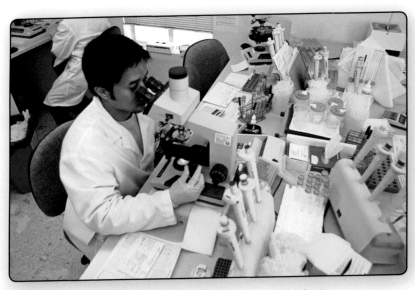

■ Sperm banks such as Cryobank prove that genetics can be big business.

Cryobank claims to be successful because it says it imposes strict standards on its donors. In addition to requiring a college education, Cryobank screens for personal health, family medical history, education, and physical characteristics. For example, donors must be at least five feet nine inches tall. On its website, Cryobank claims to accept less than 1 percent of the men who apply to be donors.

Cryobank is a business, plain and simple, and it makes a big effort to market its product. Customers can search its catalog based on characteristics such as height, weight, hair color, eye color, and ethnic origin. Advanced search options include degree and major. Customers who are willing to pay an additional fee can get the results of a personality test that describe the donor's character type. Cryobank even compares donors to celebrities they resemble. Its website lists news stories and features on selected "Donors of the Month."

Cappy Rothman, a doctor and cofounder of the firm, says his company is just giving the customer what she wants. According to Rothman, the ideal sperm donor is six feet tall, with brown eyes, blond hair, and dimples. This isn't a decision by Cryobank, it's what sells. If customer tastes should change, Cryobank would be happy to change its donor requirements. Rothman says, "If our customers wanted high school dropouts, we would give them high school dropouts."

Donor 12235: Mama's Little Surfer
"This 6' tall, blue-eyed water-lover is outgoing and fun. Traveling the world in search of great waves, his heart is always at home with his mother. Immensely proud of her and the sacrifices she made for him throughout his life, he has inherited her altruistic nature and is glad to be able to help others start their families."
From the Cryobank website

The price of genes

The Human Genome Project, which sequenced the complete human genetic map, cost hundreds of millions of dollars. Genetic information from many donors was assembled into a complete **sequence**. In 2007 the project sequenced the DNA of James Watson. Since Watson was one of the men who first explained how DNA works in reproduction, he was a natural candidate for sequencing. The cost was $2 million.

Over the past few years, the cost of analyzing human genetic structure has dropped dramatically. In 2008 a California lab called Applied Biosystems sequenced a genome for $50,000. It took only two weeks, compared to the years needed for the Human Genome Project. Later that year, another company, Complete Genomics, announced that it would be charging only $5,000 for genetic sequencing by 2009. Complete Genomics set a goal of sequencing 1,000 genomes within a year. Some genetic scientists predict customers will soon be able to buy a complete genome sequence of themselves for less than $1,000.

This drop in cost is significant. If learning about your personal genetic makeup costs $5,000 rather than $50,000, more people may take advantage of the service. And your own genome indicates what genes you might pass on to your children. As Gregor Mendel discovered, tall pea plants may still have genes for short pea plants in their genome. Similarly, a parent with brown eyes may still carry genes that would result in a child with blue or green eyes. If both parents have their genome sequenced, they have an idea of what they are bringing to the "genetic mix."

WHAT DO YOU THINK?

If you could afford it, would you have your genome sequenced? Why or why not?

As costs continue to drop, it seems more and more likely that prospective parents will take advantage of PGD services. Instead of screening embryos for defects, couples will screen their own genomes before any eggs are fertilized. From their own genetic mix, they could then select which traits they choose to pass on to their child. This raises the question of the kind of traits parents should be allowed to select. Should they only be screened for genetic defects, or should all traits be available?

■ Scientists use a DNA sequencer to analyze a sample of a client's blood or tissue.

The genetic divide

In recent years, there has been much discussion of the "digital divide" between rich and poor. Technology is expensive, and not everyone has equal access to it. Many poor families don't have a computer at home. They may depend on schools and libraries for Internet access, and poor communities may not even have that. They certainly don't have the money to spend on the variety of mobile devices available to those with higher incomes. Many wealthier families take all of this for granted.

Some people fear a similar division between the rich and poor will develop as a result of new genetic technologies and services. They call this a genetic divide.

These critics point to the many social divisions between the rich and the poor already present in society. They worry that developments in genetics will allow wealthy parents to buy genes that will give their children better abilities, such as making them smarter or stronger. The rich will have access to technologies that the poor can't afford, and this will give them an even greater advantage.

In his book *Remaking Eden*, Lee Silver, a molecular biologist at Princeton University, imagines a world in which society splits into two camps: the "GenRich" and the "GenPoor." People with enough money will create GenRich children, while the rest of the world remains GenPoor. Silver takes this idea to the extreme and sees the development of two or more human populations, separated by their designer genes. These groups will be so different that they will no longer even breed with one another. They will be two **species**.

Other people aren't as concerned about a genetic divide. They point out the advantages that wealthy parents already provide for their children. They can send them to better schools and, if the kids struggle, hire tutors. They send them to tennis camp or ballet school to improve their physical abilities. They enroll them in special courses to prepare for their college entrance exams. So these people say that providing an unborn child with genetic enhancements is no different than providing a living child with the best that money can buy.

Countries with a national health service, such as the United Kingdom and Canada, may control some of these genetic enhancements based on which procedures they will cover financially. Many European countries already have strict regulations on reproductive procedures, such as gender selection. At present, the United States has far fewer restrictions, and this is unlikely to change. As genetic science continues to advance, wealthy families may simply choose to travel to those countries that offer the services they seek. This will lead to an even greater divide between rich and poor.

■ Some people see a future in which those with enhanced DNA and those without it will be like two different species.

Whose life is it?

There's an underlying issue to all these debates that we have yet to address directly. It's the question of the rights of parents versus the rights of their children, especially those yet to be born.

Critics argue that genetic selection puts the desires of the parents ahead of the rights of the child. They say that a child designed through genetic selection is created to meet the needs of the parents. They fear that the ability to choose our children's genetic makeup makes us consumers first and parents second.

There is an additional concern that genetic manipulation may lead parents to have unreasonable expectations of their children. The parents may have arranged to have a smart child, but there are no guarantees with genetics and if the child doesn't succeed, then they become upset because they invested money and didn't get what they wanted. This is a form of "buyer's remorse," in which consumers are disappointed with a product they purchase. In this case, though, that product is their own child.

The view is even worse from the children's point of view. It may be difficult for them to tell the difference between their own achievements and those for which they have been "programmed." Since their future was decided at conception, they may feel there is no need to even strive.

Bill McKibben is an environmentalist and writer who regularly publishes articles in the *New York Times* and the American magazines *Harper's* and *Atlantic Monthly*, among others. His book, *Enough: Staying Human in an Engineered Age*, examines the future of human development in the light of new technologies. In the book, he writes, "If I am a world-class runner, but my parents inserted the 'Sweatworks2010 GenePack' in my genome, can I really feel pride in my accomplishments? Worse, if I refuse to use my costly genetic endowments, will I face relentless pressure to live up to my parents' expectations?"

Even in our current world, many children feel pressured to live up to their parents' expectations. How much worse will that pressure be for children whose genes have been chosen for them?

WHAT DO YOU THINK?

How would you feel if you knew your parents had chosen your genes with a specific future in mind for you? For example, what if they chose to give you musical ability, but you had no interest in performing music? Would you feel that you had disappointed them? Is this situation different from simply not following the path your parents might want for you?

■ In the future, will the only sports stars be those who were genetically programmed to excel?

CASE STUDY

Zain Hashmi

Zain Hashmi was born with a rare blood disorder that keeps his body from making the substance that carries oxygen through the bloodstream. By the time he was three years old, he required daily iron treatments. However, these treatments were slowly poisoning his body.

Zain could be saved by a **bone marrow** transplant, since that's where blood cells are created. But finding a good genetic match is always difficult, and Zain's doctors had not been able to find a donor. His parents, Raj and Shahana Hashmi, went to Britain's Human Fertilisation and Embryology Authority (HFEA) to get permission to create a new child specifically to save their son's life. In the United Kingdom, cases involving embryo screening through PGD require permission of the HFEA.

The procedure would involve creating several embryos and testing them to find one that was a good genetic match for Zain. The embryo would be implanted into Shahana's womb. When the baby was born, doctors would take **stem cells** from the umbilical cord and inject them into Zain. Stem cells can grow bone marrow, which Zain badly needed.

Word of the case started a firestorm. A group called CORE (Comment on Reproductive Ethics), which believes all embryos should be protected, said it was the equivalent of creating a baby for "spare parts." Zain's family claimed their son also had a right to life and that a matching embryo could save him. The case set off a legal battle, with the family and their doctors on one side, and the critics on the other.

The courts eventually sided with the Hashmi family. Unfortunately, even though they created the embryos, Shahana was never able to bring a baby to term. The family still searches for a suitable bone marrow donor for Zain.

■ Zain Hashmi's parents tried to have a child specifically to donate genetic material that would cure his blood disorder.

Savior babies

The case of the Hashmi family illustrates the concept of "**savior babies**." In this case, the parents used PGD to help a child who was already sick. The savior baby is conceived as a source of genetic material to help cure the older child. Since the two children are similar genetically, there is a greater chance that the body of the sick child will not reject the new material. In Zain's case, his parents hoped to have a child whose stem cells would help Zain grow bone marrow. In other cases, savior babies are seen as a possible future source of tissue or even organ donation.

Savior babies represent a very controversial use of genetic science. Opponents argue that no child should be created simply to save the life of an existing child. Supporters point out that this may be the only way to save a sick child. In addition, they argue that parents will love the new child as much as they would if that child had been conceived through more traditional means. The issue is still hotly debated.

Where do you stop?

The arguments against savior babies are often called "slippery slope" arguments: If you allow one thing today, it will lead to something worse down the line. Those who oppose genetic selection may have a legitimate concern. Their fear is that, in the long run, the decision won't be the choice of the parents after all. They worry about societal pressures for everyone to have children that fit some sort of social norm.

Will parents feel pressure from friends and relatives to use pre-implantation genetic diagnosis? What traits will be acceptable? Will parents feel they should avoid having children who are too short or are prone to be overweight? And if parents don't use PGD, will children who don't fit the societal norm feel like second-class citizens?

One danger of designing children to fit a social norm is that the norm is always shifting. Take weight as an example. In the past, people who were overweight were seen as successful because they had enough money to eat as much as they wanted. Today "thin is in," and people will go to great lengths to lose weight, or at least to appear slender. Because we associate youth with beauty, some people go so far as to inject Botox—a poison—under their skin to erase wrinkles. In other cultures, old age is associated with wisdom. Parents who choose genetic traits for their baby based on what is popular today may end up with a child who is no longer considered attractive in 20 years.

"When you move away from diseases, who's to say what's the better trait? Is it better to be red-headed than it is to be brown-haired? Is it better to have freckles or not? Those sorts of things are subjective and in some ways driven by our culture."

Dr. Arthur Caplan, director of the Center for Bioethics at the University of Pennsylvania

A few years back, geneticist James Watson addressed the issue of genes and intelligence. He told *The Times* of London, "The lower 10 percent who really have difficulty, even in elementary school, what's the cause of it? A lot of people would like to say, 'Well, poverty, things like that.' It probably isn't. So I'd like to get rid of that, to help the lower 10 percent." Watson later clarified that he wasn't speaking about eliminating the lower 10 percent, but about modifying their genes to make them more intelligent. Still, such thinking reminds many of the eugenics practices of the early twentieth century, in which people who were perceived as "unworthy" were sterilized. It takes control away from the individual and gives it to government.

■ Ideas about beauty change constantly. What is attractive to parents today may not be attractive to their children when they grow up.

Who says what's normal?

The idea of a social norm—whether for beauty or intelligence—leads naturally to the question of what is normal and what is not. Many people object to the idea of designing human beings based on artificial social values.

Homosexuality is a characteristic that is often at the center of the debate over social values. Some scientists believe research will eventually find a genetic explanation for human homosexuality. Such a discovery would no doubt lead to a debate over how to treat that information. Is homosexuality an "abnormal" condition? Should it be treated as a genetic disorder? Should parents be allowed to choose an embryo that does not have the genes for homosexuality? On the other hand, should parents be allowed to choose an embryo specifically because it does carry the genes for homosexuality? Behind all these questions is the fact that many genes only indicate conditions that *may* arise in the child. If a child carries the genes for homosexuality, it doesn't mean that the child will display those tendencies later in life.

Watson said that if a gene for homosexuality were discovered, a woman should be free to abort a fetus that carried it. He later qualified his statement to say that he didn't mean to single out gays. He merely meant that women should be free to abort fetuses for any reason related to genetic preference—for example, if the child would be dyslexic or lacking musical talent or too short to play basketball. But should a mother abort a child just because he won't play in the band?

■ James Watson's views on genetic science frequently draw heated responses from those both in favor and against genetic selection.

CASE STUDY

RNID

In 2007 the Royal National Institute for Deaf and Hard of Hearing People (RNID) issued a statement that deaf parents should be allowed to select the embryo of a deaf child over one who had all its senses intact. Such an act would be contrary to the Human Tissue and Embryos Bill, which was working its way through the UK Parliament at the time. That bill made it illegal for parents to choose an embryo with an abnormality if healthy embryos existed.

The RNID accused the bill of being discriminatory, because it gave parents the right to create a child free from genetic conditions while banning couples from deliberately selecting a baby with a disability. Activists claimed that there is a cultural identity in being born deaf and that deaf parents should be allowed to have a deaf child.

Francis Murphy, chairman of the British Deaf Association, said that "if hearing and other people are allowed to choose embryos that will be 'like them,' sharing the same characteristics, language and culture, then we believe that deaf people should have the same right."

■ Award-winning physicist and author, Stephen Hawking, says he's had an amazing life despite his fight with the a disease called ALS. If genetic selection becomes the norm, will society risk losing the contributions of people whose talents cannot be predicted before birth?

POSSIBLE FUTURES

Screening embryos for desirable traits is one thing. But what happens when parents have the ability to add genetic enhancements to their children? Should we have the ability to program our children for higher IQs or a longer life?

Genetic science isn't likely to stop with simply choosing traits already present in embryos. We already have the ability to alter and even add genes to organisms. In 2007 researchers at Cornell University in New York created the first genetically modified human embryo when they added a green **fluorescent** protein to an embryo left over from an in vitro fertilization. The procedure was performed simply as an experiment, and the embryo was destroyed five days later. Still, their work opens the door to new possibilities of genetic modification.

Genetic engineering

Scientists have been altering the genes of plants and animals for years. Plants have been genetically modified to be resistant to disease and to produce greater harvests. Some farm animals, such as cows and goats, have been manipulated so that they produce more milk or more nutritional milk.

■ Will future generations of human beings all have superpowers?

Animals have also been genetically modified to help produce cures for human diseases. For example, mice have been injected with genes that may cause Alzheimer's disease in an effort to find a cure. Genetically engineered insulin, used to fight diabetes, has been on the market for nearly 30 years.

■ Eighty-nine percent of the soybean crop in the United States has been grown from genetically modified seeds.

CASE STUDY

Wintergreen E. coli

E. coli is a strain of bacteria that is very popular for laboratory work because it grows quickly and is easy to manipulate. Unfortunately for lab technicians, E. coli smells really bad. More specifically, it smells like feces. So when researchers are working with a lot of E. coli cultures, the lab smells like a poorly kept bathroom.

Students at MIT decided to tackle this problem head-on. They introduced a gene from another organism—the petunia plant—to create a new strain of E. coli that smelled like wintergreen.

Encouraged by their success, they took the experiment a step further. They implanted a second gene that triggered a change in the smell once the culture was done growing. The fully grown culture smells like banana.

Some genetic engineering involves implanting genes from one species into another. In one case, researchers injected a spider gene into the genome of a goat in order to create a new material. Spider silk is very strong and, if produced in enough quantity, could create a very powerful type of body armor. Scientists discovered that the protein in spider silk is similar to goat milk. When the spider gene is inserted into a goat, the goat produces a protein that is identical to that found in spider silk. This protein is extracted from the goat's milk to produce silk fibers, called BioSteel, which is used to make bulletproof vests.

■ Spiders' webs are made from extremely strong silk.

The genes go on

Gene therapy has been used to treat genetic disorders since the 1990s. In **somatic gene therapy** (*soma* means "body"), healthy genes are inserted into a patient's body. These genes are often introduced using a specially designed virus, which then "infects" the cells with healthy genes.

Another form of gene therapy is called **germline gene therapy**. Germline cells are reproductive cells, such as eggs and sperm. Germline gene therapy alters the DNA of these cells by introducing new genes directly into the cell.

Germline therapy is already being performed on animals. For example, mouse embryos have been injected with genes that affect the growth of rats. The resulting mice grow unusually large. Because the gene was introduced into the embryo, the offspring of the altered mice will also grow larger than normal mice. The resulting animal is a new breed—a super mouse.

While germline gene therapy has not been approved for use on humans, many people fear it will be. They believe scientists will go beyond screening embryos for traits and will actually introduce new ones. For example, parents may choose to have the genes that control intelligence implanted into an embryo. In theory, it's possible that almost any trait could be added to an embryo to create a tailor-made child.

In his book *Remaking Eden*, Lee Silver introduced the term **reprogenetics** to refer to the merging of reproductive and genetic sciences. Unlike eugenics, which seeks to get rid of undesirable genes, supporters of reprogenetics want to create new and more desirable genes. They see a future in which genes are specifically created in a lab to be inserted into embryos. And since embryos are germline cells, these new genes would be carried on to new generations.

ONE EGG, THREE DONORS

In 2008 British scientists at the University of Newcastle created an embryo with three parents. Researchers removed the nucleus of an embryo created through IVF and put it inside an egg from which the original DNA was removed. The new embryo was the result of contributions from one man and two women.

The procedure was an experiment aimed at battling diseases of a cell structure called **mitochondria**. Mitochondria provide energy for the cell. When they are damaged, they can lead to conditions from liver failure to blindness. The procedure removed the healthy chromosomes from a fertilized egg with damaged mitochondria. An egg cell with healthy mitochondria had its chromosomes removed. The chromosomes from the sick cell were then placed into the healthy one. The resulting cell has material from two egg cells and one sperm cell.

Scientists are debating other possible uses of the procedure. Some see it as a possible way for homosexual couples to create a child using their own genes. The genetic material from each parent would be combined in a new egg cell. This science is still in the future.

Beyond humanity

In the wake of these advances in genetic science, a new philosophy has appeared: **transhumanism**. Transhumanists see humankind as being in transition, from human to "posthuman." Though transhumanists trace their roots back to the 1950s, the movement arose as a philosophy in 1990.

Transhumanists embrace the latest developments in genetic engineering. Rather than seeing these developments as frightening, they see humankind on the border of a new existence.

A common complaint against pre-implantation genetic diagnosis and other reproductive technologies is that they are "unnatural." Transhumanists see such a view as limited. They say that "we cannot decide whether something is good or bad simply by asking whether it is natural or not. Some natural things are bad, such as starvation, polio, and being eaten alive by intestinal parasites. Some artificial things are bad, such as DDT poisoning, car accidents, and nuclear war."

Rather than shying away from a genetically modified future, transhumanists embrace it. They accept that scientific advances will not be put on hold. Rather than rejecting new developments in genetics, transhumanists argue that we must explore them. Only then can we determine which are worth pursuing.

WHAT DO YOU THINK?

Many of the transhumanists argue against government control of technology. Is it important for government to regulate new technologies? Or can we only learn the value of new technology by using it?

CASE STUDY

Dr. James Hughes

James Hughes is one of the leaders of the transhumanist movement. He received his doctorate in sociology from the University of Chicago and currently teaches at Trinity College in Hartford, Connecticut. From 2004 to 2006, Hughes served as the executive director of the World Transhumanist Association.

Hughes has proposed what he calls "democratic transhumanism," which combines the democratic tradition of liberty, equality, and self-governance with a belief in reason and scientific progress. For him the movement is based in both technology and politics. He argues that people are afraid of technology. Because of that, technology rules them. Hughes opposes government control of technology, which he says stifles freedom. The goal of democratic transhumanism is to use technology to improve the conditions of life.

Hughes developed his ideas in his 2004 book, *Citizen Cyborg: Why Democratic Societies Must Respond to the Redesigned Human of the Future*. The book argues that a fear of technology is fundamentally opposed to democratic values. He argues that human rights are not unchanging, but that they develop and change with a changing world.

What will you do?

The issue of designer babies is your issue. At present, much of the science we've discussed is still in its infancy. In ten years, perhaps when you are thinking about starting a family, some of today's experiments will have turned into practical applications. By 2020, researchers are likely to have discovered the genetic roots of many conditions, such as diabetes, heart disease, and even psychiatric disorders. This will create an even wider interest in screening embryos for these disorders and will encourage new controversy over the ethics of designer babies.

As should be clear by now, there are no easy answers to the questions surrounding designer babies. Many techniques that were developed for their practical applications can have negative side effects. For example, for parents who carry the gene for **hemophilia**, which mainly affects males, the ability to choose not to have a boy may be a blessing. But Dr. Jeffrey Steinberg lets his patients select the gender of their child for whatever reason they choose. It brings to mind the old popular tune, "Tea for Two": "We will raise a family, a boy for you, a girl for me." On the other hand, one could argue that the decision of Steinberg's patients is personal and no one else's business. In the end, many of these issues come down to matters of personal choice.

The short story "*BD* 11 1 86," by American author Joyce Carol Oates, is about a young man who has a series of odd experiences on the day of his high school graduation. Through the course of the story, he discovers that he was conceived as a body donor. At the end of the story, he is "harvested," and another man's brain is implanted in his skull. Though the story is fiction, the scenario is one that some see as the ultimate result of creating designer babies.

Today we can only guess at what the future holds. New breakthroughs in science are happening every day. As new developments happen, scientists, members of government, and ordinary people rush to keep up. In the opening chapter, the book *Brave New World* is mentioned. The title comes from *The Tempest*, by William Shakespeare. In that play, a character remarks, "Oh brave new world, that has such people in it!" You are growing up in a brave new world. The decisions you—and others like you—make will decide what kind of people it has in it.

Genetic breakthroughs in the past 50 years	
Date	**Development**
1952	Francis Crick and James Watson make a model of the DNA molecule.
1957	Arthur Kornberg produces DNA in a test tube.
1978	Louise Brown is conceived through in vitro fertilization.
1984	Gender selection of embryos is developed.
1990	An international team of scientists begins mapping the human genome.
1990	**Gene therapy** is used on patients for the first time.
1991	Human Fertilisation and Embryology Authority is established.
1994	The FDA approves the first genetically engineered food, FlavrSavr tomatoes.
1997	Dolly the Sheep, the first adult animal clone, is born.
2003	The human genome is completely sequenced.
2009	Fertility Institutes announces plans to screen embryos for hair, eye, and skin color.
2009	Nadya Suleman gives birth to octuplets as a result of IVF.
2010	Robert Edwards is awarded the 2010 Nobel Prize for the development of human in vitro fertilization therapy.

■ In the 50 years since Watson and Crick examined the structure of the DNA molecule, genetic science has grown tremendously. It is impossible to imagine what the next 50 years will bring.

DEBATE THE ISSUES

"It's the ultimate shopping experience: designing your baby."

Jeremy Rifkin, Foundation on Economic Trends

"If I've got a dozen embryos I could implant, and the ones I want to implant are the green-eyed ones, or the blond-haired ones, that's an extension of choices we think are perfectly acceptable—and restricting them a violation of our [reproductive rights]."

James Hughes, transhumanist

"We get accused of playing God. But doctors who perform life-saving surgeries play God every day."

Dr. Jeffrey Steinberg, director of the Fertility Institutes

Making up your own mind

The three quotes above serve as a starting point for forming your own opinions about the genetic selection and manipulation that leads to "designer babies." As we've discussed, there are no right or wrong answers to these issues. How you think and feel about the issues comes from your own experience and your own point of view. How would you describe the opinions of Jeremy Rifkin, James Hughes, and Jeffrey Steinberg? Which comes closest to your own views? Why?

Recent news

On October 4, 2010, British scientist Robert Edwards was awarded the 2010 Nobel Prize in Medicine for his work developing the process of in vitro fertilization. His partner in developing the process, Patrick Steptoe, was not eligible for the award because he died in 1988. In giving the award, the Nobel committee said, "Approximately four million individuals have so far been born following IVF. Many of them are now adults and some have already become parents. A new field of medicine has emerged, with Robert Edwards leading the process all the way from the fundamental discoveries to the current, successful IVF therapy. His contributions represent a milestone in the development of modern medicine."

Monsignor Ignacio Carrasco de Paula, a spokesman for the Catholic Church on issues of bioethics, disagreed with the award. He said that, "In the best of cases they (fertilized **embryos**) are transferred into a uterus but most probably they will end up abandoned or dead, which is a problem for which the new Nobel Prize winner is responsible." Though Monsignor Carrasco stressed that he was speaking for himself, his opinion highlights the conflict the Catholic Church has with IVF.

Rights of the parent	Rights of the child
IVF procedures help millions of couples have children.	IVF procedures have destroyed millions of embryos.
Government should regulate reproductive science.	Government regulation interferes with free choice.
Doctors should be able to provide their patients whatever services are available.	Doctors should show restraint in offering services.
People should be able to buy and sell reproductive cells, just like anything else. They are personal property.	Some things should not be available on the market.
Pre-implantation genetic diagnosis helps doctors screen embryos for genetic disorders.	PGD destroys embryos which may not develop the disorder.
PGD should sort for physical traits, as well as disorders.	Unwanted physical traits should not be treated as disorders.
Gender selection helps parents avoid giving birth to a sick child.	Sex selection is sex discrimination.
People should be able to take advantage of whatever medical procedures they can afford.	New genetic technologies run the risk of increasing the gap between rich and poor.
Savior babies offer new hope to sick children.	Children should not be conceived to provide spare parts.
Embryos should be screened for abnormal genes.	Who decides what's normal?
Germline gene therapy has the potential to do away with genetic disorders.	Germline gene therapy has the potential to create a new human species.

■ The ethical issues raised by genetic selection and manipulation are difficult ones. Most of the developments that people argue against began as positive applications. In many cases, the question is where—and how—to draw the line.

GLOSSARY

artificial insemination method of introducing sperm into the female reproductive organs, other than by intercourse. Unlike in vitro fertilization, artificial insemination takes place inside the body.

bioethics field that is concerned with ethical issues surrounding developments in biology

bone marrow spongy tissue inside the bones. Blood cells are created in bone marrow.

chromosome coiled piece of DNA that contains many different genes. Chromosomes generally occur in pairs.

conceive become pregnant; when an egg cell is fertilized by a sperm cell

consumer person who buys goods and services for his or her own use

cryobank facility that collects and stores sperm to be used in artificial insemination

culture in biology, the nutritional substance on which cells are grown

DNA basic genetic material of all living things

embryo living being from conception to birth

engineer person who designs and builds things. Genetic engineers manipulate and modify genes.

eugenics movement that sought to improve the human gene pool through selective breeding and sterilization

Fallopian tubes structures in the female reproductive system that carry eggs from the ovaries to the uterus

fluorescent glowing, usually with a bright color

gene single unit of heredity found on a chromosome

gene therapy method of treating disease or disorders by exchanging a healthy gene for a defective one

genetics study of genes and heredity

genome all the genetic information necessary to build a living being

germline gene therapy form of gene therapy in which genes are introduced into reproductive cells, such as eggs, sperm, or embryos

hemophilia rare blood disorder in which the blood doesn't clot properly

infertile unable to reproduce. Infertility may be due to damaged reproductive cells (egg and sperm) or damaged structures in the body.

in vitro fertilization process by which an egg cell is fertilized by sperm outside the body

mitochondria part of the cell that turns food into energy

natural selection in evolution, the idea that positive traits are carried on because plants and animals with those traits are more likely to survive and reproduce. Also called "survival of the fittest."

octuplets eight babies who are born at the same time

ostracize exclude from a group; eject from society

pre-implantation genetic diagnosis screening embryos created by in vitro fertilization before they are implanted in the uterus

reprogenetics term coined by Lee Silver that refers to the merging of reproductive and genetic technologies

savior baby child created to "save" an older sibling who is ill, usually by contributing genetic material

sequence in genetics, the order of genes within a strand of DNA. This term may also be used as a verb and means to discover the order of genes within a strand of DNA.

somatic gene therapy form of gene therapy in which new genes are introduced into living creatures

species group of closely related organisms capable of mating with each other

stem cell type of cell in the human body that can grow into a range of different kinds of cells

sterilize make a living thing incapable of reproducing

surrogacy arrangement where a woman agrees to become pregnant and then deliver her child to another person

trait characteristic of an organism. Traits are carried by genes and may be passed from one generation to the next.

transhumanism movement that supports using science and technology to improve the mental and physical capacities of human beings

womb woman's uterus

FURTHER INFORMATION

Books

Garreau, Joel. *Radical Evolution.* New York: Broadway, 2006.
Garreau examines the implications of new genetic developments.

Glover, Jonathan. *Choosing Children: Genes, Disability, and Design.*
New York: Oxford University Press, 2008.
A short, readable overview of the issues involved in reproductive technology.

McKibben, Bill. *Enough: Staying Human in an Engineered Age.*
New York: St. Martin's Griffin, 2004.
A response to new genetic technologies, from germline engineering
to cloning.

Naam, Ramez. *More Than Human: Embracing the Promise of Biological Enhancement.*
New York: Broadway, 2005.
A positive look at how technology may change what it means to be human.

Picoult, Jodi. *My Sister's Keeper.* New York: Washington Square Press, 2005.
A popular young adult novel about a young girl who is born as a savior baby.
(There's also a video version of My Sister's Keeper, Warner Home Video, 2009.)

Sandel, Michael J. *The Case against Perfection: Ethics in the Age of Genetic
Engineering.* Cambridge, MA: Belknap Press of Harvard University Press, 2009.
An extended version of his Atlantic Monthly article of the same name. Despite
the title, Sandel does a good job of presenting both sides of the arguments.

Schultz, Mark. *The Stuff of Life: A Graphic Guide to Genetics and DNA.*
New York: Hill and Wang, 2008.
A basic guide to genetics, presented in a graphic novel format.

Websites

http://kidshealth.org/teen/diseases_conditions/genetic/genes_genetic_disorders.html

A good site that provides basic information on genetics and genetic disorders and treatments.

http://museum.thetech.org/ugenetics/eyeCalc/eyecalculator.html

A fun, interactive calculator that predicts the odds of eye color. Links explain the genetics behind how eye color is determined.

www.ornl.gov/sci/techresources/Human_Genome/home.shtml

This information page for the Human Genome Project presents background on the project, currents news, and information about ethical, legal, and social issues.

http://humanityplus.org/

The website of the transhumanist movement, includes links to Twitter pages. This organization also publishes h+ magazine at http://hplusmagazine.com/.

www.facebook.com/ieet.org

This is the Facebook page for the Institute for Ethics and Emerging Technologies, which discusses human response to a variety of developing technologies.

INDEX